W9-ATF-102

DATE DUE

15.95

977.8
Tho

Thompson, Kathleen.

Missouri

STECK-VAUGHN
PORTRAIT OF AMERICA

Missouri

15.95

Steck-Vaughn Company

Executive Editor	Diane Sharpe
Senior Editor	Martin S. Saiewitz
Design Manager	Pamela Heaney
Photo Editor	Margie Foster
Electronic Cover Graphics	Alan Klemp

Proof Positive/Farrowlyne Associates, Inc.
Program Editorial, Revision Development, Design, and Production

Consultant: Steve Kappler, Public Relations Manager, Missouri Division of Tourism

Published by Raintree Steck-Vaughn Publishers, an imprint of Steck-Vaughn Company.

A Turner Educational Services, Inc. book. Based on the Portrait of America television series by R. E. (Ted) Turner.

Cover Photo: St. Louis Gateway Arch by © Ron Thomas/FPG International.

Library of Congress Cataloging-in-Publication Data

Thompson, Kathleen.
    Missouri / Kathleen Thompson.
       p. cm. — (Portrait of America)
    "Based on the Portrait of America television series" — T.p. verso.
    "A Turner book."
    Includes index.
    ISBN 0-8114-7345-7 (library binding). — ISBN 0-8114-7451-8 (softcover)
    1. Missouri—Juvenile literature. [1. Missouri.] I. Portrait
of America (Television program) II. Title. III. Series: Thompson,
Kathleen. Portrait of America.
F486.3.T46 1996
977.8—dc20   95-49530
                                            CIP
                                            AC

Printed and Bound in the United States of America

1 2 3 4 5 6 7 8 9 10 WZ 98 97 96 95

Acknowledgments
The publishers wish to thank the following for permission to reproduce photographs:
P. 7 © Superstock; p. 8 Missouri Historical Society; p. 10 J. M. C. Photo; pp. 11, 12 Missouri Historical Society; p. 13 Library of Congress; pp. 14 (both), 15, 16, 17 (both), 18 Missouri Historical Society; p. 19 AP/Wide World; p. 20 Mark Twain Home & Museum; pp. 21, 22 Missouri Division of Tourism; p. 23 Mark Twain Home & Museum; p. 24 © Donovan Reese/Tony Stone Images; p. 26 Anheuser-Busch; pp. 27, 28 © Andrew Sacks/Tony Stone Images; pp. 29, 31 (both) Missouri Division of Tourism; p. 32 © Frank Oberle/Tony Stone Images; p. 34 Missouri Division of Tourism; p. 35 (top) The Saint Louis Art Museum, (right) Missouri Division of Tourism; p. 36 (top) Missouri Division of Tourism, (bottom) Coal Miners' Museum; p. 37 © Doris DeWitt/Tony Stone Images; pp. 38, 39 © Renato Rotolo/Gamma Liaison; p. 40 USDA Forest Service; p. 42 © Superstock; p. 44 © Ron Sherman/Tony Stone Images; p. 46 One Mile Up; p. 47 (left) One Mile Up, (center, right) Missouri Division of Tourism.

STECK-VAUGHN

PORTRAIT OF AMERICA

Missouri

Kathleen Thompson

A Turner Book

RSVP

RAINTREE
STECK-VAUGHN
P U B L I S H E R S

The Steck-Vaughn Company

Austin, Texas

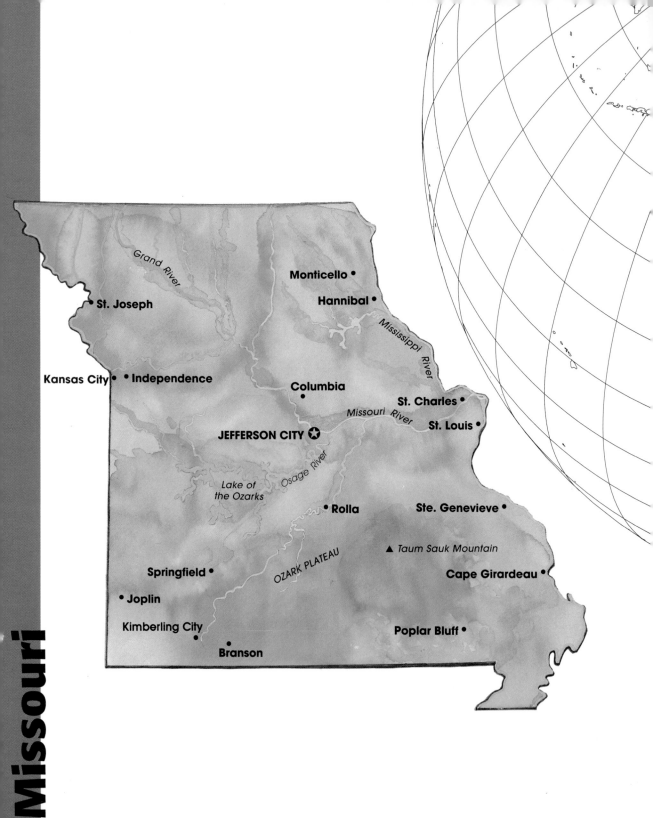

Monticello •

Hannibal • •

St. Joseph •

Grand River

Mississippi River

Kansas City • • Independence

Columbia
•

St. Charles •

Missouri River

St. Louis •

JEFFERSON CITY ⭐

Osage River

Lake of the Ozarks

• Rolla

Ste. Genevieve •

▲ *Taum Sauk Mountain*

Springfield •

OZARK PLATEAU

Cape Girardeau •

• Joplin

Kimberling City
•

Poplar Bluff •

Branson
•

Missouri

Contents

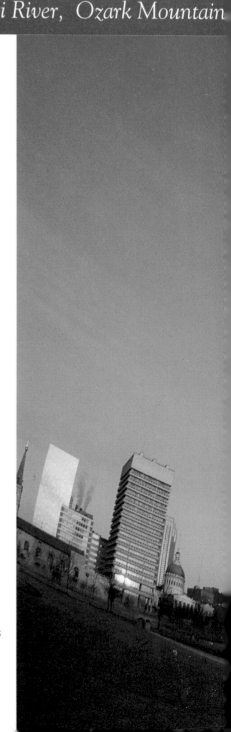

Introduction

Missouri, near the geographic center of the United States, has always been at the center of the nation's growth and progress. Missouri once served as both the endpoint of the industrial East and the starting point of the undeveloped West. Later, it was the center of political differences that divided the North and the South. Today, the state's major waterways, railways, and airlines have made Missouri into a hub of national and international travel and shipping. Missouri's central role in the making of America has extended to shaping the country's future.

St. Louis' Gateway Arch honors President Thomas Jefferson's role in the Louisiana Purchase and symbolizes Missouri's history as the gateway to the West.

Missouri

t. Louis, *the Show Me State, Mark Twain*

*W*here the West Began

Thousands of years ago, as early as A.D. 700, a group of people archaeologists call the Mound Builders lived in present-day Missouri. They were called that because they built large earthen mounds, which they used in ceremonies and as burial sites. By the time European explorers began arriving in the Missouri region, these Native American groups had divided into smaller groups. Among them were the Osage, the Sauk, the Fox, and the Missouri. Some groups continued the mound-building tradition. Most lived in permanent villages. They fished from the numerous rivers, hunted deer and small game in the abundant forests, and grew crops such as beans, squash, and corn.

In 1673 Father Jacques Marquette, a Catholic missionary, and the trader Louis Jolliet explored the upper half of the Mississippi River, including the coast of present-day Missouri. Nine years later, René-Robert Cavelier, Sieur de La Salle, explored the entire length of the Mississippi River. He claimed the land west of the river for France, including the Missouri region.

René Auguste Chouteau helped to establish the fur-trading post that later grew to become St. Louis. Chouteau was a fur trader, merchant, and territorial leader.

9

He called the land Louisiana, in honor of France's King Louis XIV.

French trappers and explorers followed La Salle to the Missouri region. Most were looking for gold and silver. Instead, valuable lead and salt deposits were uncovered. Lead was used for ammunition, and salt was important for preserving meat and fish. In the early 1700s, Antoine de la Mothe Cadillac began mining for lead in what is now Madison County.

In about 1700 French missionaries established the Mission of St. Francis Xavier near present-day St. Louis. However, the land was swampy and infested with disease-carrying mosquitoes. Many of the settlers became ill and died, and the mission was abandoned in

Bolduc House is a restored French colonial house in Ste. Genevieve, the oldest town in Missouri.

1703. In 1735 settlers established the first permanent European settlement in Missouri. It was called Ste. Genevieve and was located north of the St. Francis Xavier site.

In 1762 France transferred rights to the Louisiana Territory to Spain. Two years later Pierre Laclède Liguest and his 14-year-old stepson, René Auguste Chouteau, established a fur-trading post at what is now St. Louis. Trappers delivered furs by way of the Missouri and Mississippi rivers from as far away as present-day Montana and northern Minnesota.

Most of the settlers in the Missouri region were French, along with some people from Virginia, Kentucky, and Tennessee. In 1799 Daniel Boone led a group of settlers into the Missouri region at the request of the Spanish regional governor. The governor rewarded Boone with 850 acres of land near present-day Defiance. Boone later brought more settlers and received additional acreage.

In 1800 Spain returned the Louisiana Territory to France, and three years later, France sold the territory to the United States. In 1804 President Thomas Jefferson sent Meriwether Lewis and William Clark to explore the territory and look for a water passage to the Pacific Ocean. The expedition traveled west along the Missouri River, starting from its junction with the Mississippi.

In 1812 the United States Congress established the Missouri Territory. Native Americans watched as more and more of their land was taken over by settlers. The tensions between the two groups resulted in

This engraving depicts Daniel Boone with his dog and his favorite rifle, which he called Tick-Licker. Daniel Boone was an expert marksman and hunter.

This is a nineteenth-century drawing of three Osage Native Americans. After signing away their land in the treaty of Portage des Sioux, the Osage moved to a reservation in Kansas.

Native American raids on the settlements. After three years of fighting, the Native Americans and the federal government signed a peace treaty at Portage des Sioux.

Around 1818 a national debate was beginning to heat up concerning slavery in the United States. At that time the United States was admitting states on the basis of whether or not the state accepted slavery. Each time a state petitioned for statehood, the issue arose whether or not it would permit slavery. Many northern states did not believe in slavery. Southern states, however, insisted they needed slaves to plant and harvest cotton, their main crop. When Missouri requested statehood in 1818, the country had an equal number of "free states" and "slave states." So in 1820 the United States Congress passed a bill known as the Missouri Compromise that would settle the issue. Missouri was admitted as a slave state to balance the admission of Maine, a free state. In addition, it was agreed that no future state north of Missouri's southern border would allow slavery. Congress made Missouri the twenty-fourth state on August 10, 1821.

Also in 1821 François Chouteau of the American Fur Company established a settlement at present-day Kansas City. The company bought the furs being sent along the Missouri River to St. Louis. Soon the American Fur Company controlled almost all of the fur trade in the western United States.

Just south of Kansas City was Independence, Missouri, which was the starting point of the Santa Fe Trail. This trail linked Missouri to the territories in the Southwest. In the 1830s and 1840s, other trails, including the Oregon and California trails, linked Independence and the West. Independence thrived as a way station for goods traveling to or arriving from the West.

The slavery issue arose again in 1854, when Congress passed the Kansas-Nebraska Act. The act voided the terms of the Missouri Compromise. It stated that territories could determine by vote whether they wanted to allow slavery. The people of Kansas voted against slavery. This made Missouri's proslavery citizens feel threatened. Some reportedly slipped across the river and voted in Kansas, hoping to build a majority of proslavery votes. Many also felt threatened by changes occurring within Missouri. New settlers were arriving from northern states as well as from European

Thousands of settlers traveled west in Murphy wagons.

The Dred Scott decision voided the Missouri Compromise and was one of the events that led to the Civil War.

countries. Most of these people were against slavery. The debate in Missouri intensified.

Things became even more tense in the late 1850s during the trial of Missouri slave Dred Scott. When Scott's owner died in Illinois, a "free state," Scott went to court seeking his freedom. News of the trial in Missouri was followed very closely throughout the nation. In 1857 the final decision was left to the United States Supreme Court, which ruled against Dred Scott. The Court ruled that Scott was property, and the Constitution protected property rights everywhere in the United States. Therefore, the Court ruled, slavery should no longer be restricted, and each state could decide whether or not to allow slavery. The decision overturned all previous laws and compromises regarding slavery in the United States.

In 1861 Abraham Lincoln became President of the United States. Because Lincoln was against slavery, southern states believed Lincoln would force all states to abolish slavery. Within months after the election, seven southern states withdrew from the Union and

This photo, taken October 19, 1867, shows track being laid for a railroad three hundred miles west of the Missouri River. During the 1860s railroads helped make St. Louis a thriving transportation center.

formed the Confederate States of America. Missouri held a state convention to decide whether it should also withdraw. The state was narrowly divided on the issue by this time, but the majority of Missourians voted to stay with the Union. Four other states joined the Confederacy.

When the federal government sent troops to fight against the Confederate Army, soldiers were also sent to protect St. Louis. The city was too important a trade center to risk losing it to the Confederacy. In June Missouri Governor Claiborne F. Jackson, who was a Confederate sympathizer, called out the Missouri militia to fight off the Union troops. After the Union won the first battle, the militia fled to Wilson's Creek, where it was joined by Confederate troops. There the combined forces rallied and won a bloody battle against the Union.

Most people in Missouri didn't approve of the governor's actions. In July there was another state convention, which voted the proslavery politicians and the governor out of office. A new governor was elected. Jackson didn't give up, however. He and his supporters moved south to Neosho, and in September they held a convention of their own, voting to join the Confederacy. Now there were two state governments, one Union and one Confederate. For a few months, Jackson and the Confederate troops controlled the southern part of the state. In March 1862 they were defeated by Union troops.

But the Union victory didn't end the fighting in Missouri. For the rest of the war, battles took place

Claiborne Jackson was Missouri's governor in 1861.

This photograph shows Jesse James at the age of 17. In 1882 James was killed by one of the members of his own gang.

between rebel, or guerrilla, bands of Confederate and Union soldiers and civilians. Homesteads and farms were attacked, horses and food were stolen, and buildings were burned to the ground. Neighbor was set against neighbor. Many raids took place along the Kansas-Missouri border, near Kansas City.

The Civil War ended in 1865. About 109,000 Missouri soldiers had fought for the Union Army, more than any other northern state. About 30,000 fought in the Confederate Army. And altogether, 18,000 died. The time after the war was difficult for Missourians. Some men who had fought as Confederate guerrillas became outlaws. They robbed banks, stagecoaches, and trains. The most famous group of outlaws was the James gang, led by Jesse James. The James gang terrorized Missouri for nearly 15 years after the war.

Missouri continued to grow after the war. Pioneers moving west passed through St. Louis, the last "eastern" city in the country. Kansas City was the first "western" town people saw before they entered frontier country. Transportation in Missouri expanded to include a system of railroad lines to go along with its waterways. In the 1870s and 1880s, Kansas City became a major market for the grain and cattle produced on the Great Plains.

By 1900 St. Louis was the fourth largest city in the United States. Its growth was fueled by transportation and new businesses, such as Anheuser-Busch and the Brown Shoe Company. In other areas in the state, tobacco and cotton were important crops. In 1904 St. Louis hosted a World's Fair called the Louisiana

Purchase Centennial Exposition. Over twenty million people attended. They were introduced to brand new products that came to symbolize the modern United States: ice cream cones, hot dogs, and automobiles.

In 1917 the United States entered World War I. Missouri expanded its manufacturing and farming industries to supply the armed forces. After the war, Missourians cleared large areas of forest and drained swamps to gain more land for agriculture. They also built levees and dams to control flooding and generate electricity in rural areas. In the 1920s the Tri-State Mining District near Joplin opened the largest zinc-mining district in the country. Lead mining was also profitable.

In the 1930s the country's economy was in ruins. This period is known as the Great Depression. Banks closed, farms and industries went out of business, and workers lost their jobs. Many people in Missouri left their farms and went to the cities looking for work. When the country entered World War II in 1941, the economy improved as factories undertook

above. These people are gathered for the opening day ceremonies of the 1904 World's Fair in St. Louis.

below. Many factories in Missouri manufactured weapons during World War II.

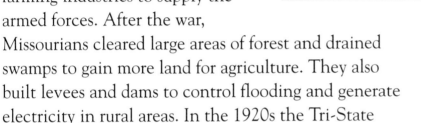

manufacturing war supplies. Kansas City and St. Louis were centers of the defense industry.

Missouri's contribution to the country during the war years wasn't limited to soldiers and defense needs. In 1945 Harry S. Truman, from Independence, became President of the United States when Franklin D. Roosevelt died in office. Many historians consider Truman one of the country's greatest Presidents.

The 1950s and 1960s were boom times all over the United States. New industries in Missouri produced electrical components and parts for spacecraft. Uranium and iron mines opened in the state.

As cities became more crowded and less safe, many people moved to the suburbs. Improved transportation allowed people to work in the cities but live in outlying towns. The movement of so many people hurt the economies of cities such as St. Louis and Kansas City a great deal. The migration out of the cities continued into the 1970s.

A number of urban renewal projects began in St. Louis and Kansas City in the 1980s. These were improvement projects for the cities that restored older buildings and built attractive downtown gathering sites. The farmlands suffered from severe environmental problems, however. As land was cleared to build homes and industries, toxic substances ran off the land and poisoned the lakes and rivers that farmers used to water crops and livestock. Even groundwater was affected. The situation was so serious at Times Beach that the federal

President Truman is holding a newspaper printed on election night, before all the votes for President were counted. When they were, Truman had won the election.

18

When this photo of the City Hall in Lupus was taken during the 1993 floods, floodwaters still had not risen as high as they eventually would. Many Missourians died or became homeless during the floods.

government bought all of the land in that area, and everyone who lived there was forced to move away.

In the late 1980s, the national economy entered a recession. Missouri needed funds for education, law enforcement, and care for the poor and elderly, so it began a state lottery. The economy was beginning to return to normal when disaster hit. In 1993 both the Mississippi and the Missouri rivers flooded after heavy rains. Most Missouri counties were declared disaster areas, and there was more than four billion dollars in property damage and crop losses.

Today, Missouri's strong economy and the continued developments in the cities provide a healthy outlook for the future. In addition, many smaller towns have contributed to and benefited from the progress of these nearby cities. Missourians are linked together in an effort to keep making progress throughout the twenty-first century and beyond.

Mark Twain and the Mississippi

Most Americans learn about the Mississippi River from a number of sources. Encyclopedias and geography books describe the river's length and width and the names of its early explorers. But no one has added a more personal touch to the river than the author Mark Twain. He once compared the mighty Mississippi to a book that had a "new story to tell every day." And Mark Twain used his writing to tell that story in his own unique way.

In the 1840s and 1850s, a few cities had been established on the banks of the Mississippi River. Here and there they sprang up, from the Canadian border to the Gulf of Mexico. Among these were St. Louis, Memphis, New Orleans, and the twin cities Minneapolis-St. Paul. Beyond the Mississippi to the west was the frontier—a vast expanse of land stretching all the way to the Pacific Ocean.

Many people in the East thought of the Mississippi River as the borderline of civilization. St. Louis, Missouri, was the hopping-off point to the Wild West. Actually, St. Louis did have a little bit of the Wild West mixed in with its big-city society. There was high-stakes gambling and livestock trading, and plenty of money was rolling through.

Mark Twain is shown in 1902 in front of his boyhood home in Hannibal.

The steamboat was the mode of transportation that linked the river towns. It was a straight-sided, flat-bottomed vessel propelled by a steam engine that drove a paddle wheel. Steamboats were used to carry goods and passengers to port towns—and even farther if they wished.

Mark Twain was born in 1835 near Hannibal, Missouri, a little more than one hundred miles upriver from St. Louis. As a young boy in Hannibal, Mark Twain loved to watch the steamboats float up and down the river. To Twain these boats symbolized freedom—and adventure.

One day he decided to find out what the view was like from aboard a steamboat. He slipped onto one of the boats while it was docked and hid

This riverboat was named after Mark Twain, whose real name was Samuel Clemens. The author took his pen name from a riverboat term, mark twain, *which means two fathoms, or twelve feet deep.*

himself under a lifeboat on the upper deck. There he thrilled to the sound of the signal bells and the smell of the churning river. It was a feeling he would want to experience again and again. Later, writing in *Life on the Mississippi*, he said, "When I was a boy, there was but one permanent ambition among my comrades. That was to be a steamboatman."

Mark Twain made that ambition a reality in 1857. At the age of 22, he boarded a steamboat called the *Paul Jones*. His original plan was to travel down the Mississippi to New Orleans. However, almost as soon as the boat set off, his old childhood excitement took hold of him. Twain engaged the captain, Horace Bixby, in conversation. During their talk Bixby allowed Twain to take the wheel of the boat. Within a short time, the two had struck a deal, and Bixby agreed to take Twain on as a "cub" river pilot. Twain spent the next two years traveling the Mississippi River route between St. Louis and New Orleans.

There was a lot to learn. Before Mark Twain signed on with the riverboat, he "supposed all that a pilot had to do was to keep his boat in the river." But under the careful guidance of Captain Bixby, Twain soon learned that the river was always changing; the ever-shifting waters of the Mississippi could be treacherous. If a pilot didn't keep careful records of the changes, the boat could strike a sandbar. The pilot was also responsible for knowing the location of submerged rocks and the wreckage of other boats. Pilots were required to keep a log book, or journal, of the river's shifts. As time went by, Twain used his log book

Mark Twain's famous characters Tom Sawyer and Huckleberry Finn are depicted in this memorial to the author in Hannibal.

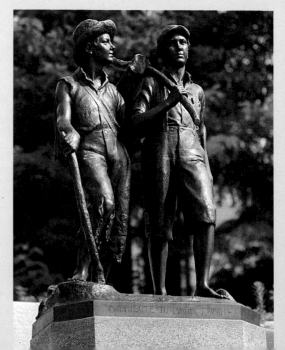

to record other things as well. In it he wrote stories and newspaper articles. Whenever he wasn't at the pilot's wheel, Twain was writing. The river was a constant source of inspiration for him.

During his training, Twain learned every bend in the river, every shallow spot, and every tiny town along the way. It was hard work, but he loved it. In 1859 Twain was granted his river pilot's license. Working on a riverboat was a happy time in Mark Twain's life, but it didn't last long. In 1861 the Civil War all but shut down riverboat traffic along the Mississippi River because the fighting made transport too dangerous.

In his writing Twain continued to use what he had learned as a riverboat pilot. Some of his books, such as *The Adventures of Tom Sawyer*, *The Adventures of Huckleberry Finn*, and *Life on the Mississippi*, show readers what life was once like on the river. The power of Mark Twain's writing brings to life one of the world's greatest waterways—the mighty Mississippi.

Across the Country in Every Direction

Near the center of the country, two rivers meet. The great Missouri curves into the mighty Mississippi. The well-watered plains north of the Missouri River provide some of the richest farmland in the country. Glacial deposits made the topsoil rich and black. They call it "mud-on-the-boots country." The rivers have also contributed to the growth of Kansas City and St. Louis. These river ports were trade centers for many of the early southern and western settlements along their routes. These cities are still thriving today, transporting goods across the country by water, rail, roads, and the air.

Manufacturing makes up 21 percent of Missouri's economy. Two thirds of manufacturing takes place in and around St. Louis and Kansas City. Missouri's most important product is transportation equipment such as automobiles, airplanes, barges, railroad cars, and truck trailers. St. Louis is the home of McDonnell-Douglas, a major manufacturer of military and commercial aircraft.

The J. C. Nichols Fountain in Kansas City commemorates the man who built the Country Club Plaza, the world's first shopping center.

25

Chemicals are Missouri's second largest manufacturing product. Chemical products include medicines and paints as well as agricultural chemicals such as pesticides and fertilizers. Food processing is also an important manufacturing activity. Springfield has one of the largest dairy processing plants in the country, producing butter and cheese products. Beer is a product of processing grains, hops, and other ingredients. Anheuser-Busch in St. Louis is the largest brewer in the world. In addition, Kansas City has a number of large mills that process grain into flour.

Although agriculture only makes up about three percent of Missouri's economy, farms cover about two thirds of the state. In the fertile hills of northern Missouri, farms produce corn and soybeans. There are ranches on the flat, rocky prairies of southwestern Missouri. That is where beef cattle, dairy cattle, sheep, and hogs are raised. The "boot heel" region in

St. Louis-based Anheuser-Busch employs a team of Clydesdale horses as its company symbol. This Clydesdale team is pulling the Anheuser-Busch wagon in a parade.

Missouri ranks second in hog production in the United States.

southeastern Missouri has rich soil that's also good for growing soybeans and cotton. All over the state, farmers produce grapes, apples, and peaches.

Mining contributes only one half percent of Missouri's economy, but it is still important. Missouri ranks first in the country in mining clay, lime, and lead. Missouri is also a source of coal and silicon sand which is used to make glass. Other minerals produced in Missouri include crushed limestone, clays, barite ore, and coal.

The largest part of Missouri's economy—about 72 percent—involves services. People who work in the service industry don't make products. Instead they serve people. The biggest service category in Missouri is community, social, and personal services. In this category are people who work in professions such as secretaries, doctors, or lawyers.

The second largest service category is wholesale and retail trade. Wholesale trade mainly involves

Most Missouri farms grow soybeans, corn, or wheat. Soybeans are the state's most profitable crop.

selling goods in large amounts, usually to companies and stores. Retail trade involves selling smaller quantities of goods, usually to individuals. Wholesale trade is very important in Missouri. Much of the wheat and other grain products produced in the Midwest are stored in the grain-storage facilities in Kansas City. Companies that need grain in large amounts purchase it from those storage areas. Kansas City also has the largest wholesale livestock business in the country.

The third most important category of services is finance, insurance, and real estate. This category includes banks, insurance companies, and businesses that help people buy property.

The fourth largest category of Missouri's service economy is transportation. This category is important for moving crops and other agricultural products from farm to market. It also allows raw materials to be moved in and finished products to be shipped out. Missouri has a strong system of roads and railroads.

Every year railroads carry between three to four million carloads of freight. Missouri air traffic—both passenger and freight—covers the country. The state also has a highly developed river transportation system.

The last category of the service economy is government. These are city, state, or federal services. Workers include teachers, police officers, and firefighters, as well as state and federal park employees and elected officials. Military bases also fall into this category.

The Ozark Mountain region in southeastern Missouri is a place of great natural beauty. It has become the focus of Missouri's very profitable tourism industry. Tourism is very strongly tied to Missouri's service economy, bringing in more than $14 billion a year. Visitors from all over the country come for hiking, cave exploring, camping, boating, and many other activities. Other Missouri tourist attractions include the Six Flags Over Mid-America theme park, paddle-wheel riverboats, and a large number of historic sites.

This blacksmith demonstrates his craft at Silver Dollar City, a theme park that re-creates turn-of-the-century life in the Ozarks. Silver Dollar City was built in 1960 and has been attracting tourists ever since.

Missouri's rich and varied landscape has allowed the state to develop a diversified economy—one in which money is made from many different sources. Missouri also enjoys a central location in the country; it borders eight states. Its ability to produce a large variety of products and ship them with ease ensures Missouri a healthy economy for many years to come.

Working on the River

The most common way businesses move their products from one place to another is by truck or train. But in Missouri, products are also shipped by river barge. Today, St. Louis is the busiest inland river port in the United States. About 218 million tons of cargo are conveyed through this port every year.

Barges are large, flat structures designed to carry mostly bulk freight such as grain, coal, steel, petroleum, and cement. In most cases several barges are lashed together. Then they are pushed along the river by a tugboat. A typical crew on a tugboat includes several barge workers, a cook, and a captain or "river pilot."

River pilots are specially trained and licensed. Whether they work on the Missouri River or on the Mississippi, they have a respect for flowing water. One pilot on the Missouri described the challenges: "The Missouri River is probably one of the most hazardous rivers in the western river system to run, as far as swift-ness and current. Sandbars will build quite frequently and blow out (break down) just as fast. So you really have to keep up-to-date on this river. It's a hard river to learn." Pilots have to know the river, and they also have to be able to "read the water." That means they have to recognize the signs that signal that a sandbar has built up, shifted its position, or completely disappeared. The pilot continued, "The river moves. It changes. . . . A man cannot completely memorize the river." The safety of the crew and the cargo depends on a pilot's ability to be very alert to a river all the time.

Most people who work on the river spend their entire lives doing this kind of work. Part of the appeal is the beauty of rivers. One pilot described the most beautiful time on the river as . . . all the time. But most people find it hard to explain. Maybe it's magic, because one river worker could only explain it this way: "River people'll tell you that if you ever work on a boat long enough to wear out a pair of shoes, you'll never quit. And that's it. The river gets in your blood."

The Army Corps of Engineers is responsible for keeping the channel in the Missouri River at a depth of nine feet, so that fully-laden barges can travel down the river with few troubles.

The Ste. Genevieve-Modoc ferry is one of the last of its kind in the United States. The ferry carries vehicles and passengers across the Mississippi River between Missouri and Illinois.

From Upscale to Down-Home

Missouri has a strong cultural tradition. The state has produced writers, painters, and musicians who are known all over the world. It has symphony orchestras and schools of the dramatic arts that are considered some of the best in the nation. Culture in Missouri is vital and very alive.

Probably the most famous Missouri writer is Mark Twain. Twain's books were based on his experiences growing up in Hannibal, Missouri. Twain is often thought of as one of America's greatest humorists and writers.

Missouri has produced other well-known writers. T. S. Eliot, who was born in St. Louis, is considered to be one of the best modern-day American poets. Eugene Field wrote well-known children's poems, or nursery rhymes. Among his verses are "Wynken, Blynken, and Nod" and "Little Boy Blue."

Missouri is also the proud home of fine musicians and musical styles. Ragtime music composer Scott Joplin moved to Sedalia as a young man and enjoyed

The Climatron greenhouse is part of the Missouri Botanical Garden in St. Louis, which is home to more than 12,000 kinds of plants from all over the world. The Climatron houses tropical plants.

33

great success with "Maple Leaf Rag" and other songs. The Ragtime Archives Collection in Sedalia honors Joplin's music. Ragtime music was popular in the United States in the early 1900s. It is characterized by a steady rhythm and irregular accents. Ragtime music was part of the origin of American jazz. Kansas City, Missouri, is a center of jazz music. Count Basie was a Kansas City jazzman who became an international star. Every year jazz history is celebrated in the 18th and Vine Heritage Festival in Kansas City. Missouri's tradition of making popular music continues in Branson, the new center of country and western music.

Missouri also claims two of America's greatest painters. Thomas Hart Benton painted lush and sometimes startling pictures of the Missouri landscape. He also painted ordinary people in scenes of everyday life. George Caleb Bingham was famous for his paintings of river life in the Midwest.

Another Missourian who has had a tremendous influence on American art as well as the American

This boy is playing the piano in Sedalia's annual Scott Joplin Ragtime Festival. Scott Joplin is known as the "Father of Ragtime."

This is Thomas Hart Benton's painting, "Cradling Wheat." In the 1920s and 1930s, Benton helped to lead the American Scene movement in American art.

imagination is Walt Disney. Disney created America's most beloved animated characters—Mickey Mouse and Donald Duck. His full-length films are considered classics of animation. When Disney built Disneyland in California, he based its Main Street on the one in his hometown of Marceline.

Missouri's culture is certainly rich and varied. The St. Louis Symphony Orchestra is the second oldest orchestra in the country. The Coyote's Paw Gallery features fine arts and crafts from Africa, Asia, islands in the Pacific, and North and South America.

History is also a major part of the culture in Missouri. For example, the pony express, founded in 1860, had its headquarters in St. Joseph, not far from Kansas City. Every year St. Joseph holds Pony Express Days, which let people see a reenactment of the mailmen of the early West. People in Kearney can visit the

The pony express (1860–1861) was a mail service from St. Joseph, Missouri, to Sacramento, California.

The Onondaga Cave at Leasburg is only one of the five thousand caves in Missouri.

Jesse James Birthplace and Museum. Jesse James, his brother Frank, and the rest of the James gang have become legends in the history of the American West.

Pioneer life is represented in Missouri's history exhibits. The Log House Museum in Lexington includes a restored log home that was built in the 1830s. The museum shows the life and hardships of early pioneers. The National Frontier Trails Center in Independence is dedicated to the importance of the Santa Fe, Oregon, and California trails in the development of Missouri and the American West. All through the state, there are Civil War monuments and museums, such as General Sweeny's Museum of Civil War history, near Springfield.

Various groups of people who have played important roles in Missouri's history are also celebrated. Early French explorers and fur trappers are honored by museums and festivals in Ste. Genevieve. This is the home of the earliest European settlements in Missouri. German settlers who came to Missouri before the Civil

The Coal Miners Museum in Novinger displays clothing and mining equipment from Novinger's days as a prosperous mining town.

The Nelson-Atkins Museum of Art in Kansas City is one of the largest art museums in the United States. The giant sculptures on its front lawn are badminton shuttlecocks.

War are honored in museums and festivals in Hermann and Westphalia.

Every state has festivals during the year, but only in Missouri will you find National Tom Sawyer Days. One of the most popular Tom Sawyer contests is the National Fence Painting Championship, in honor of the task Tom Sawyer hated so much. In Eureka the seed-spitting contest is an essential part of the town's Watermelon Festival. Columbia hosts the State Championship Wild Turkey Calling Contest. Many Missouri counties hold rodeos and fairs throughout the year.

Missouri has an enormous number of things to see and experience. A variety of historical and hands-on activities are available. Most of all, Missouri reflects the lifestyles of the cities and the farms. It is a state that grew up on Midwestern values: common sense, moderation, and good clean fun.

Branson: Country Music Capital of the Universe

Does the sound of a bluegrass guitar send shivers down your spine? Does the cry of an old-time fiddle reverberate from your toes to your fingertips? Does the pounding of a honky-tonk piano make you want to get up and dance? If so, you might want to take your dancing feet to Branson, Missouri, which calls itself "the country music capital of the universe."

Branson is in southern Missouri, surrounded by the Ozark Mountains and deep, clear lakes. For a long time, people have headed to the Branson area to admire lush Ozark forests, to relax in the soft mountain breezes, and to listen to the waves wash up on the shore of Lake Taneycomo. Visitors have often taken a side trip to Silver Dollar City, a restored 1880s mining town, or explored Marvel Cave.

Music has also been a part of Branson. Early Ozark settlers migrated to this region from the Appalachian Mountains. They brought with them old folk songs that their ancestors had sung. Over the centuries these songs have mixed with blues, popular songs, and hymns to produce today's country music. For more than fifty years, Branson has been the home of popular country music radio programs.

There are more live entertainment theaters in Branson than in any other United States city, and the theaters have more seating than New York City's Broadway. More than five million people visit Branson every year.

Shoji Tabuchi performs in his theater in Branson. A classical violinist and country music star, Tabuchi is one of Branson's most popular entertainers.

Country music became very popular across the country in the 1980s. As a result, the musicians and the country music recording industry made a lot of money. In addition, music theater owners and advertisers also cashed in on the popularity of country music. Everybody was happy—except for one thing. As country music kept gaining more and more fans, the ticket prices kept rising. Country musician Roy Clark thought that was wrong. He believed country music was getting too expensive for ordinary people and their families to afford.

So Roy Clark went to Branson and built his own theater. That way he could be sure that ticket prices at his theater would stay affordable. Star after star followed his example. Performers such as Glen Campbell, Mel Tillis, Jim Stafford, Mickey Gilley, and Charley Pride all opened their own theaters. By 1994 Branson, a town of about three thousand people, was the home of about fifty theaters!

Other big-name country music stars came to perform there, too. The word spread quickly, and soon Branson was known as a place where the stars appreciated their fans. Today, Branson is the place where country music is making musical—and economic—history!

The Irish Wilderness

In Missouri eight large blocks of land make up the Mark Twain National Forest. One block comprises nearly 17,000 acres in Oregon County. People there call this region "the Irish wilderness," or "the Irish." It is named after a group of Irish immigrants who lived there before the Civil War. For 11 years, people in the county debated how to use the land. Should it stay a wilderness area or should it be developed by mining companies?

One person who wanted to save the Irish was Dorothy Ellis, a judge who has lived in Oregon County most of her life. "Future generations . . . should not have to go to a World Book [encyclopedia] or dictionary to look up the word *wilderness*," she said. "They should be able to experience it, just like I have."

Real estate developer Don Ross wanted to put the Irish to different

use. Four generations of the Ross family have lived in Oregon County. Ross felt that the lead deposits in the Irish should be mined. He explained his position. "We get . . . a good potential for having a mining operation here and they say, 'Oh, no, we don't want any mining in Oregon County, because it's gonna destroy the environment.' Well . . . [using resources is] the American way."

Another resource in the Irish is trees. Ellis's group appreciated their natural beauty. Ross's group saw them as a crop to be harvested. Ross pointed out that around 1900, many trees in the Irish were cut down for lumber. The trees in the Irish today were planted to replace the ones cut

The Irish wilderness in the Mark Twain National Forest is open to visitors who enjoy camping and hiking.

down. "It's ridiculous to turn this over to somebody and just let them do nothing with it," he said.

Ellis didn't think that saving the Irish was "doing nothing with it." Her group felt that people need a quiet place where they can be in touch with nature. "I don't just see the Irish, I feel it, and I think it's what a lot of people [need] to feel right now . . . We've all been in a fast lane. And I think people . . . need to get away and to have this feeling."

But the Irish couldn't be both a wilderness and a lead mine or lumber source. Finally, Ellis's group took the conflict to Washington, D.C., and the Irish wilderness became part of the Mark Twain National Forest. Now people can visit the wilderness. They can explore the caves along the Eleven Point River, which winds through the region.

The debate over the Irish is typical of debates about the environment occurring throughout the country. One group wants land preserved. The other wants to use its resources. Both sides want the best for everyone. In Oregon County, they didn't give up until the issue was resolved.

Show Me . . . the Future

Missouri is called "the Show Me State," which means that Missourians require a logical explanation or demonstration before they'll accept an idea. Today they're applying that logical, step-by-step approach to economic growth.

Missouri's economy is going strong these days, especially in the major cities where 73 percent of all manufacturing takes place. The other 27 percent is spread out over the rest of the state. Missouri wants to make sure that future economic growth includes smaller communities, too.

The method the state has agreed upon provides elements of the "show-me" philosophy for which Missouri is well known. It has established the Missouri Department of Economic Development. The job of this department is to work with communities that want to attract businesses to their location. With the department's help, a town analyzes the advantages that it can offer to a company and the kinds of businesses the town would like to attract. Then the state helps

Kansas City is Missouri's largest city and a center for commerce, industry, and transportation in the Midwest. Its success has carried Missouri to the threshold of the twenty-first century.

the town search for companies that fill the community's goals.

Why is this a good way to proceed? One reason is because the people of the town have a great deal of input in what kind of business is built in their community. Some businesses fit certain communities better than others. For example, many businesses require a minimum number of employees, or they need certain resources that the town must provide. The state provides information, procedures, and advice, when it's needed.

When towns grow in this way, many future problems are avoided. The public discussion allows the people of the town to control their growth, and by doing so, they strengthen the community.

By creating this economic development program, Missourians have exhibited a practicality that perhaps even goes beyond "show me." In fact, this program may become so successful in the future, Missouri may want to consider becoming the "Watch Me" state.

The Science Center in St. Louis has 650 exhibits on technology, ecology, the environment, the humanities, and space. Missourians are taking the time to educate themselves about subjects that will be important in the future.

Important Historical Events

1673 Father Jacques Marquette and trader Louis Jolliet reach the mouth of the Missouri River.

1682 René-Robert Cavelier, Sieur de La Salle, claims the Mississippi Valley for France.

1700 A Catholic mission is established at present-day St. Louis.

1715 Lead is discovered in the Viburnum Trend.

1719 Claude Charles du Tisne explores the Missouri River.

1735 Ste. Genevieve is founded.

1762 France gives Spain the area west of the Mississippi River.

1764 St. Louis is founded by Pierre Laclède Liguest and René Auguste Chouteau.

1799 Daniel Boone leads a group of settlers into present-day Missouri.

1800 Spain gives the Louisiana region back to France.

1803 France sells the Louisiana region to the United States.

1804 Meriwether Lewis and William Clark begin their expedition at the mouth of the Missouri River.

1812 Congress organizes the Territory of Missouri.

1815 The United States government signs a peace treaty with Native Americans at Portage des Sioux.

1819 Steamboat traffic begins on the Missouri River.

1820 The Missouri Compromise is signed.

1821 François Chouteau opens a trading post at Kansas City. The Santa Fe Trail is opened.

1826 The capital moves to Jefferson City.

1837 The United States government buys Native American land claims in Missouri.

1857 The United States Supreme Court rules against Dred Scott.

1859 The first railroad crosses the state.

1860 The pony express begins in St. Joseph.

1870 In the Great Steamboat Race from New Orleans to St. Louis, the *Robert E. Lee* defeats the *Natchez.*

1882 Jesse James, a notorious outlaw, is killed at St. Joseph.

1904 St. Louis is the home of the Louisiana Purchase Centennial Exposition.

1931 The Lake of the Ozarks is created by the construction of the Bagnell Dam on the Osage River.

1945 Missouri adopts a new state constitution.

1958 Construction is completed on the Table Rock Dam on the White River.

1965 The Gateway Arch in St. Louis is completed.

1973 The State Environmental Improvement Authority is created.

1979 The Harry S. Truman Dam is completed.

1986 Missouri establishes a state lottery.

1991 Cleanup begins on the dioxin-poisoned land in Times Beach.

1993 Every county in the state is declared a disaster area after the Mississippi, Missouri, and other rivers cause the worst floods of the twentieth century.

The state flag has three horizontal stripes of red, white, and blue, which represent loyalty to the Union. At the center is the state coat of arms, surrounded by a ring of 24 stars. The coat of arms features two grizzly bears holding a shield. The bears symbolize the state's strength and its citizens' bravery.

Missouri Almanac

Nickname. The Show Me State

Capital. Jefferson City

State Bird. Bluebird

State Flower. Hawthorn

State Tree. Flowering dogwood

State Motto. *Salus populi suprema lex exto* (The welfare of the people shall be the supreme law.)

State Song. "Missouri Waltz"

State Abbreviation. Mo. (traditional), MO (postal)

Statehood. August 10, 1821, the 24th state

Government. Congress: U.S. senators, 2; U.S. representatives, 9. State Legislature: senators, 34; representatives, 163. Counties: 114

Area. 69,686 sq mi (180,486 sq km), 19th in size among the states

Greatest Distances. north/south, 319 mi (513 km); east/west, 365 mi (588 km)

Elevation. Highest: Taum Sauk Mountain, 1,772 ft (540 m); Lowest: along the St. Francis River near Cardwell, 230 ft (70 m)

Population. 1990 Census: 5,137,804 (4% increase over 1980), 15th among the states. Density: 74 persons per sq mi (28 persons per sq km). Distribution: 69% urban, 31% rural. 1980 Census: 4,916,759

Economy. *Agriculture*: beef cattle, soybeans, hogs, milk. *Manufacturing*: transportation equipment, food products, chemicals, electric and electronic equipment, fabricated metal products, electric machinery, printed materials. *Mining*: lead, coal

State Seal

State Bird: Bluebird

State Flower: Hawthorn

Annual Events

★ National Intercollegiate (NAIA) Basketball Tournament in Kansas City (March)

★ Dogwood Festival in Camdenton (April)

★ Maifest Celebration in Hermann (May)

★ Silver Dollar City Music Festival (June)

★ National Tom Sawyer Days in Hannibal (July)

★ Fair St. Louis (July)

★ Bootheel Rodeo in Sikeston (August)

★ The Great Forest Park Balloon Race in Kirkwood (September)

★ Pershing Balloon Derby in Laclede (September)

★ American Royal Livestock, Horse Show and Rodeo in Kansas City (October/November)

Places to Visit

★ Boone's Lick State Historic Site, near Booneville

★ Climatron in the Missouri Botanical Garden in St. Louis

★ Confederate Memorial State Historic Site, near Higginsville

★ Country Club Plaza in Kansas City

★ Gateway Arch in St. Louis

★ Harry S. Truman Library & Museum in Independence

★ Lake of the Ozarks

★ Mark Twain Cave, near Hannibal

★ Meramec Caverns, in Stanton

★ Onondaga Cave State Park, near Laclede

★ Pony Express National Museum in St. Joseph

★ Trail of Tears State Park, near Cape Girardeau

Index